A Guide to
Florida Personal Injury

Sharing the Secrets, Learning the Lies

Wade Coye

I WOULD LIKE TO THANK MY WIFE JOAN,
MY DAUGHTER AUSTIN, AND
DAN SMITH II, MY LAW PARTNER,
NEIGHBOR AND FRIEND.

I AM ALSO GRATEFUL FOR THE HELP OF
LUCAS SARRIS, MY DOAN, FAYE SWEETNAM,
MARCHELLA TARR, JOSHUA WINOGRAD,
AND KEENAN SMITH.

SHARING THE SECRETS, LEARNING THE LIES
Second edition printing.

DISCLAIMER: THIS BOOK IS MEANT FOR GENERAL INFORMATIONAL PURPOSES ONLY AND IS NOT INTENDED AS LEGAL ADVICE. Each person's individual situation is different. Before taking any legal action, it is highly recommended that you consult with an attorney in your area concerning your specific circumstances.

Printed in the United States of America

ISBN: 978-1-63385-127-6

Design and publishing by:
Word Association Publishers
205 Fifth Avenue
Tarentum, Pennsylvania 15084
www.wordassociation.com
1.800.827.7903

1
Introduction

Let's face it, we're human. Accidents and injuries are going to happen at some point or another, and sometimes it is no one's fault. There are times, however, when someone has been negligent, careless, foolish, or in some way at fault. At those times, if you have had an injury, you have a "personal injury." Personal injury law is designed to protect and compensate you if you are injured or harmed because of someone else's negligence. I wrote this book to familiarize consumers about the law and to offer practical suggestions should you suffer a personal injury. As helpful as the Internet may be, fact is, there is no substitute for getting advice from a skilled and experienced personal injury attorney. Personal injury law is not a perfect system or easy to navigate, but it is the only system available to you in order to receive compensation for your unfortunate injuries or losses. To my fellow attorneys, I wrote this book to help consumers; it is not a how-to book, and I welcome feedback that will help better educate everyone about the perils and pitfalls of the personal injury system.

Wade B. Coye

Disclaimer

The materials available in this publication are for informational purposes only and not for the purpose of providing legal advice. You should contact your attorney to obtain advice with respect to any particular issue or problem. Use of and access to this material does not create an attorney-client relationship between The Coye Law Firm and the user or reader.

2
Could Your Case Be Worth A Million Dollars?

They call it "personal" injury for a reason; each person's case is different, and results vary based on a variety of factors such as the amount of medical bills, lost wages, mileage, and other expenses. Additional factors include the percentage of fault by each person involved in the case, available insurance coverage, how old a person is, and how much an injury has influenced your life.

A common question early in the case is, "How much is my case worth?" If we are discussing something like car repair, it is easy to obtain several estimates for the repair costs. However, it is rare to know the value of a personal injury case early, since it is difficult to have a complete understanding of a person's entire medical situation. The value of a personal injury case is dependent upon the extent of injuries, the amount of your medical bills, how much of your medical bills are paid by someone else, the amount of your wage losses, and how much, if at all, damages will continue to increase in the future. There are many factors, which makes this an area of great controversy.

One way to understand personal injury case value is to look at the verdict form in a typical personal injury case. First, a jury is asked whether there was negligence on the part of the defendant (the person sued) that was the legal cause of the plaintiff's (the person who filed a lawsuit) injuries or damages. This is a yes-or-no question, and if the jury says no, there was no negligence, then you have lost your case. The next question is whether there was any negligence on the plaintiff's part or any other party's part. The answer to this question could have the impact of reducing the overall amount of damages that you may recover. Next, most verdict forms are going to ask a jury to decide the total amount of the medical expenses related to the accident and the total amount of the wage loss. Another question will ask whether these injuries are permanent. If the injuries suffered in a motor vehicle accident are not permanent, then pain, suffering, and damages from the past may not be collected.

Sample Verdict Form

IN THE CIRCUIT COURT OF THE 26th JUDICIAL CIRCUIT IN AND FOR ORANGE COUNTY, FLORIDA

JAMES SCOTT

Case No. 12-2025-OR-0065

Plaintiff.

v.

Defendants.

____

VERDICT

We, the jury, return the following verdict:

1. Was there negligence on the part of the defendant which was a legal cause of injury or loss to plaintiff?

YES _____ NO _____

If your answer to question 1 is NO, your verdict is for defendant, and you should not proceed further except to date and sign this verdict and return it to the courtroom. If your answer to question 1 is YES, please answer question 2.

2. Was there negligence on the part of plaintiff which was a legal cause of his or her injury or loss?

YES _____ NO _____

3. State the percentage of any negligence or fault, which was a legal cause of injury or loss to plaintiff that you charge to:

(defendant) __________%

(claimant) __________%

Total must be 100%

In determining the amount of damages, do not make any reduction because of the negligence, if any, of (claimant) **or the [negligence]** [(specify other type of conduct)]**, if any, of** (identify additional person(s))**. If you find that** (claimant) **or** (identify additional person(s)) **[was] [were] negligent [or at fault], the court in entering judgment will make an appropriate reduction in the damages awarded.**

SO SAY WE ALL, this ______ day of ______________, 2______.

____

FOREPERSON

The value of personal injury cases are highly influenced by the amount of medical expenses and wage loss. In small cases involving minimal injuries, the insurance company sometimes will pay a small sum of money and be done with the case without very much proof of loss. In larger cases, specific proof of medical complications could be important to convince an insurance company to pay sizable damages before a lawsuit is filed with the court. Most of the time, lawyers can give you a range of the value of the case based upon their experience. Insurance companies actually keep a database of the amounts they have paid out in particular cases, which are shared with each other, but not with consumers.

The initial amount the insurance company offers for your case is not necessarily the final amount, and they may have to pay more or less in your particular situation. The important point to remember is that all of the data that is being accumulated on personal injury cases in general and over time is influencing your present case. For instance, if a person suffers a certain back injury and the insurance company typically pays $40–$60,000 for that type of back injury, that does not necessarily mean that in future cases the insurance company is going to willingly pay $40–$60,000 right off the bat. If they can pay $20,000 on a future case, they will do it. Every case is different. Nevertheless, the data accumulated from settlements and jury verdicts in similar cases are a substantial factor in the settlement values an insurance company places on your case. Remember, the insurance company is a business and is expecting to make a profit. Just because you have heard of a neighbor or friend receiving a certain amount of money for a particular

> Your case is a unique situation with its own facts, details, range of value and factors.

case does not necessarily mean that your similar case is worth the same amount. Your case may be worth much more or much less, depending upon the circumstances. It is actually unfair to evaluate your case based on what you have heard about someone else's case, be it a friend or even someone on television.

Think of your case as a unique situation, with its own facts, details, range of value, and factors that could change the outcome. So many details of your case can vary from others, such as your age, your background, your insurance company, the amount of available insurance coverage, your medical expenses, any future medical expenses . . . the list goes on, and that is just the minimum of information needed in order to evaluate your case.

Lawyers sometimes develop short descriptions of cases and may ask each other what they think is the relative value of a case by considering the many factors that I listed above. Insurance companies use extensive amounts of data that they have accumulated in past cases to make decisions about present cases. Insurance companies look at all available information from past cases as well as the unique data about your case to determine how much to pay, and to see if they can pay you less on the claim.

SECRETS AND LIES

You can evaluate your case based on someone else's case. (**Truth:** Every case is different.)

The total amount of medical expenses and wage loss is one of the most important components in determining case value. No matter how bad the defendant's conduct appeared at the time, it rarely is a factor in the total amount of the settlement.

3
Who Will Pay Your Bills? What You Don't Know Can Cost You

There are several different resources available to help you with your personal injury case. However, you may not be aware of the pros, cons, rules, and regulations that each resource has.

NO-FAULT INSURANCE

One of the more common types of injury accidents involves motor vehicles. Americans drive thousands of miles yearly and, because of this, individual states require motorists to demonstrate financial responsibility. A common question is, "Why does my insurance company have to pay my medical bills and lost wages?" The answer is because that is the law. In Florida, we are required to insure ourselves for the first $10,000 in medical expenses and wage losses we have incurred after being in a motor vehicle accident. If you own a vehicle in Florida, you are required to have no-fault insurance coverage, also called personal injury protection. No-fault insurance coverage pays 80 percent of your medical expenses and 60 percent of lost wages up to $10,000. However, no-fault insurance is more complicated than most people would think.

No-fault insurance coverage pays 80 percent of your medical expenses and 60 percent of lost wages up to $10,000.

No-fault insurance covers you, family members that reside with you, occupants of your car, pedestrians, you riding in another car or riding a bicycle, and even your child so long as the accident involves a motor vehicle. The rules involving personal injury protection are complex, particularly as they apply to recovery of medical expenses.

The first thing to understand about no-fault coverage in Florida is its limits. Once it is used, it is gone. For instance, if you were transported to a hospital via ambulance and a number of tests were run including blood work, CT or MRI scans, and you were released a short time afterwards, then a good amount of the $10,000 in available coverage is probably already used up. The first discussion I have with clients is that they should treat no-fault coverage like a line of credit. Once it is used up, you cannot access it again. If you use your coverage to pay for medical care but realize you need that money to pay for lost wages instead, you can rarely go back and tell the insurance company where you would rather use that coverage. You must notify the insurance company in the beginning that you wish to reserve the funds for wage loss, and you must notify your doctor's office and/or hospital that you need them to bill your health insurance. This can result in a bit of a conflict since doctors and hospitals generally prefer to receive no-fault benefits over other forms of payment as it pays better. Ultimately, it is your decision how to spend your no-fault coverage.

A decision about reserving no-fault benefits for wage loss is often dependent on other factors such as other available resources, impact on medical treatment, and whether the loss of income is imminent. This area requires a complete review with experienced legal counsel to maximize the resources available to you and your family. It is important to consider the totality of your needs so that you might budget accordingly. While it may seem odd to budget medical expenses after an accident, sometimes it is necessary if the resources are limited, such as with personal injury protection.

MEDICAL PAYMENTS COVERAGE

Medical payments coverage is a type of insurance that is sometimes included on homeowner policies, motor vehicle policies, and some small commercial policies. Large commercial establishments rarely have some type of medical payments coverage. It is important to determine early on after an accident if this resource exists since there are typically very limited periods to file insurance claims and to submit various bills and receipts. With this type of insurance coverage, it pays irrespective of whether or not someone is at fault.

Medical payments coverage is also sometimes available on an automobile insurance policy. It is a benefit paid in addition to personal injury protection. Medical payments coverage can pay deductibles and co-payments. If your personal injury benefits are exhausted, then you can use your medical payments coverage to receive medical care and notify the insurance company that you wish to reserve some of the personal injury protection benefits for wage loss benefits, as I referenced earlier. It is important that you have considered medical payments coverage early in a case; otherwise, medical providers could use up your personal injury protection benefits and leave you without any funds to cover your personal bills while you are medically recovering. Medical payments coverage and your personal injury protection are resources with finite amounts of coverage (remember the line of credit analogy), so it is important that you are paying attention to what you are spending your resources on at the doctor's office.

One of the unique differences between personal injury protection coverage and medical payments for motor vehicle incidents in Florida is that personal injury protection benefits do not need to be repaid if you obtain a settlement from an at-fault driver or from your uninsured motorist benefits. However, medical payments benefits that are used in a motor vehicle incident may have to be paid back. This becomes particularly important if the treatment you received was not something that the at-fault insurance company necessarily deems related to the injury. So on one hand, your insurance company may have paid your medical bills with your personal injury protection, but on the other hand, the at-fault insurance company may claim the medical treatment was excessive or unrelated. Confusing? You bet.

LETTERS OF PROTECTION

If there is no insurance coverage available to assist you in paying for various types of health care and/or wage loss, a letter of protection is needed. A letter of protection is a promise from the lawyer and the client (the injured person) to pay the doctor, clinic, diagnostic center, therapist, or pharmacy at the conclusion of the personal injury case. This means that the settlement funds received from an insurance com

> A letter of protection is a promise from the lawyer and the client (the injured person) to pay the doctor, clinic, diagnostic center, therapist, or pharmacy at the conclusion of the personal injury case.

pany have to be used by the lawyer to pay those medical providers. Unfortunately, a letter of protection does not have any bearing upon the likelihood of recovery of money in the case. There are a number of problems with letters of protection that are commonly overlooked by injured people and lawyers involved in the handling of personal injury cases.

As you may have noticed, when you go to the doctor, you are required to make a payment or show proof of health insurance before you receive treatment, not after. Among the pros of providing a letter of protection to a doctor is that first, a letter of protection allows you to obtain medical treatment where you otherwise may not be able to without health insurance or cash up front. Letters of protection can also help you protect your credit rating in situations where you have incurred medical bills from a hospital or emergency room visit. Sometimes, if medical providers are not paid following provision of services, unpaid bills are sent to a collection agency, which affects your credit rating. An additional pro is that it is easier to get appointments when you are seeing doctors who are providing care because of a letter of protection. It is also easier for your lawyer to obtain medical records and to settle the case rather quickly if it is a small amount of medical records from the same medical provider. Also, a doctor working under the terms of a letter of protection may be willing to reduce the amount of their bill depending on the case outcome.

The amount of paperwork associated with letters of protection are usually substantially less, and they can play a role in bearing how the doctor will handle the bill at the conclusion of the case. Most doctors who have provided medical care using a letter of protection are more willing to provide trial testimony, and that willingness is an important factor in the success of your case. However, if you have had to obtain medical care and treatment from a doctor utilizing a letter of protection, then you could end up with medical bills that are owed to the doctor whether or not a jury provides you with a favorable outcome.

Unfortunately, not many doctors are willing to provide medical care and treatment with a letter of protection, as it means they must wait for the conclusion of the case to receive payment or risk not being paid at all if your case is unsuccessful in obtaining a settlement. Oftentimes with a letter of protection, the final medical care and treatment cost are higher than usual because of this. Medical providers and insurance companies may already have a negotiated rate or contract; however, a doctor may charge higher rates if there is some risk of nonpayment and that up charge does not mean you will receive more money at the conclusion of your case. In addition, a letter of protection can potentially allow a medical provider a greater right to collect funds from your settlement at the conclusion of the case than would have existed if they were just using your health insurance.

The extracontractual right that a letter of protection likely confers on a health-care provider may be a consideration in avoiding such an arrangement. Letters of protection may also limit the quality of medical care you would receive, because of the nature of the type of medical providers who supply the care. For instance, some medical providers may not have hospital privileges because they have had some prior problems with meeting the required standard of care or have caused an injury to a patient and were sued. This is by no means to suggest that doctors who provide treatment using a letter of protection are not good doctors. In fact, some of the finest medical providers use letters of protection to handle the care of their patients.

A doctor may be willing to wait for their fees at the conclusion of the case, but a tricky situation occurs if they recommend MRIs and CT scans at a hospital that does not accept the letter of protection. For example, a complicated brain injury may require ongoing care and treatment from a specialist in order for any possibility of a reasonable recovery. However, it may be difficult to locate the appropriate specialist. In the end, you may be left with a doctor's recommendations but no way of receiving the treatment you need to make you well.

Insurance companies may also use a letter of protection to indicate that a doctor's testimony is influenced because they have not been paid. The doctor's testimony includes information such as the severity of your condition and necessity of future care, which may influence the overall amount of money awarded at the conclusion of a jury trial. Even a doctor's opinion, medical notes, and records, are presented as part of a settlement before trial and are examined by insurance companies. In short, doctors working under a letter of protection are not afforded the type of credibility that you may want in the final decision making of your case.

HEALTH INSURANCE

Health insurance is an important resource if you are injured and seeking monetary recovery from the at-fault person and their insurance company.

In the case of most health insurance policies, whether group policies, individual policies, or Medicare policies, there either have been or continue to be premiums paid for the insurance. Typically, as part of the arrangement of a health insurance plan, there have been negotiated contract rates with various hospitals and medical providers, and these can benefit you in a personal injury case. A common mistake is to assume that the at-fault insurance company will pay all of the injured person's medical bills. Usually there are only limited resources available from the defendant's (at-fault) insurance company, and the limitations of those resources will affect the outcome of your case.

It is important to know which medical providers are shown on your health insurance plan, as it can affect your overall case. Some providers are not necessarily interested in assisting a personal injury case, and you should identify those providers prior to beginning treatment, if possible.

> A common mistake is to assume that the at-fault insurance company will pay all of the injured person's medical bills.

All health insurance plans contain something called a "right to subrogation," which means that the health insurance plan has a right to be repaid in whole or in part from any type of settlement you may receive from an at-fault person or their insurance company. This right to subrogation, which you have agreed to whether you know it or not, is part of your insurance plan. Following an accident, your health insurance company may even send you paperwork for you to sign, which again states that you agree to repay them at the conclusion of the case.

In the event that there is some type of recovery from an insurance company, many group health plans have a right of subrogation to recover all benefits they have provided for their policyholder. This can influence the total outcome and total settlement of your case if you are partially at fault or suffer from a preexisting condition.

Your health insurance company may have a provision in your policy documents that allows them to recover 100 percent of everything they have paid in your case, even if you did not recover 100 percent of the amounts paid on your behalf. These situations can reduce the flexibility that your lawyer has in your case. It is also distressing to learn at the conclusion of your case that substantial amounts of money are owed to your health insurance company. It may feel like a lot of the work was done to benefit your health insurance company. A letter of protection could be helpful to avoid your health insurance company demanding 100 cents on the dollar that they have paid out of their policy. This is a complexity important for you to understand in connection with your case and to discuss with your lawyer.

A common problem following an accident with injuries caused by negligence is a possible disruption of income that can result in cancellation of your health insurance policy. While there may be an opportunity to continue coverage even after the loss of employment, the payment of expensive premiums can be very problematic when someone has lost their income. If you find yourself in this situation, I have found it may help to obtain a loan against your case that will pay for the insurance premiums. This way you can continue to receive the medical treatment and care you need to make a full recovery. Remember, the medical documentation that is generated after a doctor's visit is critical in order to obtain a settlement in your personal injury case.

WORKERS' COMPENSATION

Should you use workers' comp as part of your case? There are many important considerations to make.

If your injury took place while at work and your workplace is required to have workers' compensation, you may be able to use this benefit in your injury case. Workers' comp is a resource paid for by your employer and is required in most workplaces. This benefit can pay for medical care and treatment as well as some lost wages.

First, consider the type of medical care you receive and from whom you will receive it. In a workers' comp injury case, the insurance company gets to select a medical provider and is not particularly concerned whether you have a full recovery.

The insurance company adjuster's main objective for the workers' comp care is to see that you are provided the minimum care that the law requires them to pay. Your overall health and welfare are not necessarily a consideration. In fact, insurance adjusters in a workers' comp case can micromanage the type of care that their selected doctor provides. This could actually become a self-fulfilling prophecy, and the doctor may limit the amount of care they provide if he or she knows the insurance company is not going to approve the type of care or treatment requested.

The insurance adjuster may even control what prescription your doctor will give you, what test the doctors will order for you, and what procedures the doctor may provide. They may even ultimately decide if the doctors will provide any more care and treatment for you, whether you continue to suffer from injuries or not.

Therefore, a careful review of the workers' comp insurance company and doctors provided is essential when making decisions about which resource is available and how it will be used.

In situations where there is no health insurance and you have no other means of obtaining care and treatment, all you can do is make the best of the limited care that workers' comp provides you.

Workers' comp takes into account different factors such as preexisting conditions and division of fault between the parties. This may affect and lower the total amount that you are going to receive from your personal injury settlement.

Unfortunately, it is not in the interest of workers' comp carriers and claims adjusters to provide the best care possible. While there are some insurance adjusters who are sincerely interested in the well-being of an injured worker and want to assist in that person's full recovery, you should not consider the workers' comp insurance company as an entity that is representing your interest and assisting you with a full range of options and needs.

Just like health insurance plans, the workers' comp insurance company has a right of subrogation as well. This allows them to recover the benefits that they have paid on your behalf regarding your recovery. However, unlike many of the health insurance plans, the workers' comp carrier takes into account different factors such as preexisting conditions and division of fault between the parties. This may affect and lower the total amount that you are going to receive from your personal injury settlement.

When given the choice between a health insurance plan and workers' comp, it is sometimes more helpful and appropriate to use health insurance. However, this choice does not come without a cost; if you did not receive care or treatment from workers' comp, then the workers' comp carrier does not necessarily have to pay for the lost time benefits that may accrue under the workers' comp law.

Keep in mind, when considering whether to use workers' comp benefits for your medical care, there are specific notice provisions in the law. For instance, in Florida your employer must be notified within 30 days that you have suffered some kind of job injury. This can be a trap to those unaware that the absence of a formal injury notification can create additional problems. This is an example of why sometimes it is vital to seek counsel from an experienced lawyer early in the case.

MEDICARE AND MEDICAID

Resources that are often overlooked are various government programs. The typical government program is Medicare, a federal-level insurance plan that is provided because you have been paying premiums in connection with your work. You are eligible for Medicare if you have reached full re

> If you are expected to be disabled for a prolonged amount of time, you should apply immediately through the Social Security Administration website: www.ssa.gov.

tirement age; or if you find yourself disabled under the Social Security disability system, then you can become a Medicare beneficiary after a two-year waiting period.

Depending on the nature of the injury, you may be able to qualify for "private disability." If your injury causes a disability for more than a year, you may qualify for a closed period of disability benefits. If you are expected to be disabled for a prolonged amount of time, you should apply immediately through the Social Security Administration website: www.ssa.gov.

When Medicare is available to an injured person, there are typically no limits to any type of doctor, hospital, or diagnostic center. Most medical providers accept Medicare, given the size of the program.

Since most individuals of retirement age are Medicare recipients, you can imagine the tremendous number of medical providers in the United States that accept Medicare. Just like health insurance carriers and workers' comp carriers, Medicare also has a right of subrogation.

According to Medicare, the payments made to care for you after an injury are called "conditional payments," and Medicare has a legal right under federal law to be repaid the funds they have paid to care for you from a settlement you received.

In the last several years, an additional complication has developed with respect to receiving care and treatment using Medicare. Although Medicare has its benefits, sometimes the difficulty in satisfying Medicare's lien (right to subrogation) interest, as well as satisfying the insurance company's anxiety over how the Medicare system operates, can cause substantial delay in the settlement of your case. If you are a Medicare recipient, Medicare needs to be placed on notice if they are providing any funds to medical providers that you have seen following an accident, because some insurance companies insist to receive proof from Medicare that nothing has been paid or that provision has been made to pay the amounts actually paid. Medicare makes a conditional payment, when an insurance company may be ultimately responsible.

If you do not place Medicare on notice, then a substantial delay will occur at the conclusion of your case. Medicare has an absolute right to recover the funds it pays to various medical providers on your behalf—from you, your lawyer, and the insurance company. Medicare considers itself a secondary payor in injury cases, which means that they are not obligated to pay your medical bills if there is other insurance available. Medicare's interest must also be taken into account with respect to any ongoing care and treatment that is needed at the conclusion of the case. Presently, Medicare is still developing rules and regulations for how this is supposed to take place and how they will implement this aspect of the law. Medicare has the right to be paid the money that they have already paid out, and they do not expect to pay for any future care or treatment when someone else is paying you money for that future care and treatment.

Medicaid is a poverty-level program that provides very basic treatment and is administered by the individual states. For instance, Medicaid can pay for hospital bills, some diagnostic tests, and some ongoing care by authorized doctors within its plan. Most people who have experienced an accident or injury find Medicaid very frustrating when attempting to receive care and treatment.

Emergency room visits are not a problem, but follow-up care with the doctor can be difficult. Much like Medicare, health insurance plans, and workers' compensation, Medicaid also has a right to subrogation. Failure to repay Medicaid the money that was paid on your behalf following receipt of a settlement can result in criminal penalties. Most people find that Medicaid is only useful in the most extreme injury claim situations, because of the limitation of doctors who are willing to accept it.

SECRETS AND LIES

SECRET You can choose when and where to use your $10,000 in no-fault coverage. However, once you use it, it is gone.

LIE You can keep your whole settlement. (**Truth:** You may have to repay some to your insurance company.)

SECRET If you are hurt at work, you must notify your employer within 30 days of the accident.

SECRET If you want to use Medicare, place them on notice immediately, or else a substantial delay will occur. There are no limits to Medicare, and most medical providers accept it.

SECRET Pros of using a letter of protection:

- It is easier to get appointments.
- It can protect your credit.
- It is easier to gather medical records and there is less paperwork.
- The doctor may lower his or her bill

depending on the case outcome.

- The doctor is more willing to provide trial testimony, which could be crucial to your case.
- It helps your case to show that you have many medical bills.

Cons of using a letter of protection:

- Some bills may be higher because of the risk of nonpayment.
- It could limit the quality of medical care because of the of the medical practice that accepts them.
- It allows medical providers a greater right to collect funds than if they only were paid from health insurance.
- The doctor may send you for tests at different centers that do not accept letters of protection.
- Insurance companies will imply that the doctor only says you are sick because the doctor wants to be paid.

- Some doctors working under a letter of protection are not afforded credibility by the insurance industry.

(Notwithstanding the pros and cons, my office routinely sends clients to doctors who provide treatment with a letter of protection, as many injured people do not have health insurance.)

4
Why Your Case Is Only as Good as the Available Insurance Coverage

When someone is in an accident, particularly a motor vehicle accident, there is a common belief that the at-fault person should pay for all of the damages. Many of our clients become frustrated when they learn that full coverage in Florida does not necessarily mean the at-fault person has available insurance money to pay for any bodily injuries caused in a motor vehicle accident.

Florida does not require drivers to carry bodily injury coverage. As a result, there are many accidents in Florida where the at-fault person and their insurance company may not have to pay anything for your injuries. If you have been in an accident, it is important to examine all available options for insurance that will pay for the damages you have suffered. This exploration of available insurance companies is usually one of the first matters that a law firm may undertake on your behalf. Typically, if you are injured in a motor vehicle accident, there is an effort to examine the insurance coverage for the at-fault driver, the owner of the vehicle of the at-fault driver, or any other insurance coverage that may be available.

If the at-fault driver does not have bodily injury coverage, then you may have to look to your own uninsured motorist coverage to make an insurance settlement.

UNINSURED MOTORIST COVERAGE

In the event that the at-fault driver does not carry any bodily injury coverage, uninsured motorist coverage is specifically designed to provide you with a source of recovery. Complete reviews of your insurance policy along with any waivers that you may have signed for your insurance coverage are important parts of evaluating your personal injury case.

UMBRELLA COVERAGE

Umbrella coverage is a type of insurance policy that provides coverage in addition to the basic amounts of coverage that a person may carry.

> Florida does not require drivers to carry bodily injury coverage. As a result, there are many accidents in Florida where the at-fault person and their insurance company may not have to pay anything for your injuries.

PREMISES COVERAGE

Premises liability insurance is insurance that protects a landowner or premises owner from claims of negligence against them. Homeowners and businesses have a duty to make sure their property is reasonably safe and to caution visitors of any existing dangerous conditions.

If you are injured at someone's home or business due to some defect on the premises, then you could make a claim

On a premise liability claim you must be able to show:

- ✔ The property was in a dangerous or defective condition.
- ✔ The owner or person in possession of the property knew or should have known about the dangerous or defective condition.
- ✔ The owner or person in possession of the property had time to repair or warn of the condition but did neither.
- ✔ The dangerous or defetive condition caused the injury.

against the homeowner or business. Their premises liability coverage will normally pay for any injuries you sustained. However, just because you somehow fall or trip on someone's premises does not mean that person is responsible for your injuries and damages. You cannot just trip and collect a settlement; someone must be negligent in order for you to make a recovery on a premises case.

EMPLOYER'S COVERAGE FOR INJURIES CAUSED BY EMPLOYEES

Some accidents may involve an employee who is driving a company vehicle or driving their own vehicle while on company business. If an employee on the job injures you, then that employee's company may be responsible for your injuries.

This is why it is important that all details of an accident be investigated. For instance, if someone was driving his or her own personal vehicle and caused an accident injuring you, it is important to determine, prior to concluding that there is no available insurance coverage, whether that person may have been on the job when the accident happened.

SECRETS AND LIES

LIE — The at-fault person will cover all of your bills. (**Truth:** They may not have enough coverage, and you may be left with your own bills.)

SECRET — If the at-fault driver does not have insurance, sometimes there is uninsured motorist coverage.

SECRET — If you are injured on someone's property, look into premises coverage.

SECRET — Find out if the person who hurt you was on the job.

5
Dealing with Doctors: Secrets That Can Make or Break Your Case

Now that we have talked about how much your case is worth, what resources you might have, and the different types of coverages, let us talk about some problems that can occur involving your injury and going to the doctor.

It goes without saying; if you are hurt, go to the doctor. For accidents where there are ambulances or immediate trips to the hospital to save a life or limb, going to the doctor or emergency room may not have been your decision to make. If your injuries were the result of someone's negligence, you need to educate yourself on your rights, the limitations of the law, and mistakes to avoid. It is here where consulting a lawyer can provide you the experience and expertise to get you the justice you deserve within the law.

Many times, insurance companies will attempt to have a severely injured person sign a release and issue a minimal check jointly to the victim and the hospital. It would be in your best interest to contact a lawyer *immediately*, before you sign anything.

> In Florida if you do not receive medical care within 14 days of an accident, then your no-fault insurance company may not have to legally pay any of your bills.

If an injury you have suffered has resulted in sizable bills, a common mistake is to assume that someone else will be paying the bills. Too often, the injured person learns too late that certain resources must be used in a timely manner; otherwise, they may not be available. For example, in Florida if you do not receive medical care within 14 days of an accident, then your no-fault insurance company may not have to legally pay any of your bills.

Very serious injuries, even if properly diagnosed, require follow-up medical care. This is important from a medical standpoint, but for purposes of your personal injury case, the quality of the care and the records developed can be critical in recovering money for the injuries you have sustained.

Many times after visiting the emergency room, the medical staff will recommend follow-up care with different types of medical doctors. Patients will often follow up with their care only to learn that the doctor will not accept their health insurance; or even worse, the patient does not have health insurance. In this case, the doctor may choose not to see the patient or may even indicate in the medical file that the injury was not serious and discharge them from care. Enormous legal issues ensue when a doctor writes a medical report that does not accurately represent the current medical situation, which is the possible result of a concern that they would not be paid.

Does it happen? Absolutely! So what can you do to receive and pay for the medical care you need?

Sometimes, patients and lawyers do not consider the importance of a proper medical referral following the initial hospital or urgent care center visit. It is vital to discern the type of follow-up care as it relates to your specific personal injury case. The consequences may be extremely detrimental to your health and your case. Your health insurance company is not necessarily providing you with a list of doctors who will be helpful with your personal injury case. Therefore, as a patient, you should do extensive research and seek out proper guidance before going to a doctor.

First, if you have been discharged from the hospital with recommendations for follow-up care, the selection of the doctor is so important that you may want to consult with a lawyer. Although hiring a lawyer at this stage may be the last thing you want to do, it is an option. Good lawyers know the range of medical professionals in an area and usually know which doctors are comfortable testifying in legal situations on health insurance and doctors who do not wish to participate in the legal system. Personal injury lawyers also know which doctors may not have strong credibility with the insurance company. You can imagine the problem in your case if your doctor has no credibility. Avoiding this problem can be as important as the medical treatment you receive.

Second, if consulting with a lawyer is not possible right away, and you have health insurance of some form, you should check to see which doctors are on your list and do a bit of research about a particular doctor. A simple call to their office to ask if they handle personal injury patients should suffice. You would be surprised how many doctors are not interested in treating injury victims if they believe the legal system will be involved. Some doctors may even blame your medical issues on something other than your accident if they do not wish to participate in your legal case. Hospitals and your health insurance company will not differentiate between doctors that will or will not treat injury victims when they refer the case for follow-up care. Your primary focus is whether the doctor has the professional credentials to provide the care, such as an orthopedic surgeon, neurosurgeon, plastic surgeon, etc. Rarely

> You would be surprised how many doctors are not interested in treating injury victims if they believe the legal system will be involved.

will the hospital or your health insurance company differentiate between different types of orthopedic surgeons and neurosurgeons. Even within these specialty areas, there are subspecialties that can make a difference in how your medical care is received. For instance, if you have a shoulder issue, an orthopedic surgeon who specializes in shoulders and who has received advanced training in this area may be the best doctor to treat you. If you are referred to a general orthopedic surgeon, then while they may be able to handle your care, they may not have the specific training, background, and expertise to recognize and treat some very specific injuries. Injuries can heal quicker when corrected early. Additionally, receiving the most accurate doctor and specialized care can substantially influence the amount of money that is recoverable and the bills that are paid in your case.

If you have been referred for follow-up care from an accident and you do not have health insurance, your options are very limited. If you are faced with this situation, you may need to immediately consult a lawyer to see what options are available in order to receive timely medical care. As I discussed in chapter 3, in some very limited circumstances, there are doctors who are willing to provide medical care with a letter of protection. However, this is by no means an optimal situation.

As I also mentioned, if you are provided medical treatment with a letter of protection, the insurance companies might attempt to diminish the value of the doctor's professional care. The insurance company will insinuate to a jury that the doctor's opinions are biased since they will only be paid if the jury forces the defendant (insurance company) to pay money for the case.

It is rare that an insurance company will find the billing to be legitimate and fair, suggesting oftentimes that the billing is somehow inflated and too high for the facts and circumstances of the case. Even though the treating doctor is trying very hard to care for their patient and is certainly taking a risk by caring for someone without the promise of immediate payment, the insurance company will still use the doctor's goodwill in a negative manner. Letters of protection are also used to cover the patient's deductible that exists on many health insurance plans and on many no-fault policies. This can help injured people whose resources may already be strained due to absences at work from pain, limitations, or doctors' appointments.

Overall, it is not advisable to enter into a letter of protection arrangement with a medical provider without legal counsel. While the doctor may be willing to provide the care, other considerations need to be discussed and understood. This is not to say that letters of protection are inherently bad, only that they come with certain concerns.

Medical payments, health insurance, and letters of protection are problematic if you require follow-up care and do not have any remaining no-fault coverage. At this time, you should examine whether you may be immediately eligible for some other form of health insurance. I have participated in several cases in which an individual did not have health insurance for a variety of reasons. Perhaps the premiums were too high or the individual simply had not considered purchasing health care in the past. Either way, getting health care immediately may still be possible and could assist with your medical needs as well as your legal case. If premiums are too high for your present budget, then sometimes it is possible to arrange a loan against the financial outcome of your case that can be used to pay the premiums on health insurance. This step must be carefully considered and evaluated for its strengths and weaknesses. For instance, you may discover that the enrollment period for a particular policy has passed or that it is too far in the future for you to avail yourself. You may also determine from a review of the policy that there are specific exclusions for preexisting conditions, such as the injuries you have sustained.

These specificities make up a very complex area of insurance law and I do not recommend you make any final decisions without the benefit of a lawyer. Each insurance policy is different, and their rules can affect the outcome of your case. Borrowing money using your personal injury case as collateral requires a complete understanding of the complexities of your case, understanding of health insurance policy law, some appreciation for your specific medical condition, and consideration of costs and expenses.

Follow-up care can also be obtained under limited circumstances by borrowing money using your case as collateral. This is a bit of a hybrid between the letter of protection and borrowing to pay health insurance premiums. There are some companies established to loan in very specific cases and circumstances, and a limited number of doctors who will work with these companies. The costs and expenses of this particular type of an approach can be substantial and should only be used in a very limited number of cases—such as when there have been very specific recommendations for medical procedures like surgeries on joints or neck or back injuries, and there is either not enough insurance to induce the doctor, surgical center, and/or hospitals to provide the procedures needed. If you believe this is an approach worth considering, then understanding your specific medical issue, the liability in the case, causal relationship, available insurance coverage, likelihood of settlement versus suit, and whether the case is likely to settle prior to trial are but a starting point.

PROBLEMS IF YOU DO NOT GO TO A DOCTOR

There are decisions that could have a very negative impact on your personal injury case if you are injured in an accident and do not visit a hospital or doctor at once. If you have an injury and seek payment from the person at fault, then you must start with having this injury properly documented. Simply getting into an accident and asserting that some body part is injured is insufficient. Many times, a person's case is only as good as the medical documentation; therefore, you must document the injuries, no different than documenting the damage to your car if you were in a motor vehicle accident.

> If you have an injury and seek payment from the person at fault, then you must start with having this injury properly documented. Many times a person's case is only as good as the medical documentation.

Insurance companies look to various data points after an accident to make a determination of value. For instance, how long was it after the accident until you went to the doctor? Of course, this is not always an accurate portrayal as to whether someone is seriously injured. For instance, I was raised on a dairy farm where it did not matter how hurt you were or how much pain you had, the cows needed to be fed and milked. For my dad and grandfather, unless an injury was so bad that they could not physically work, they were not going to the doctor. If a doctor's appointment were made (no doubt at the insistence of my mother or grandmother), it might be scheduled in a week or so, but clearly not after there was substantial delay. Continuing to work with an injury could result in a more serious injury and claims from the insurance company that "if it hurt so badly, you would have seen a doctor."

The delay you make in getting your injuries documented will be used against you. To an insurance company, delay in treatment means either there is nothing wrong with you or something else happened that led you to go to the doctor. The insurance company will not give you points for sucking it up or pat you on the back for being tough. Even worse, as I mentioned before, if you are in a car accident and do not go to the doctor within 14 days, you may not be able to use the no-fault benefits that you have paid for. There is nothing wrong with choosing to delay or avoid going to the doctor, so long as you recognize that your delay will not help you medically and most certainly will be used against you legally.

SECRETS AND LIES

SECRET

In Florida, if you do not go to the doctor within 14 days, the insurance company may not have to pay your bills. In addition, if you delay in going to the doctor, the insurance company might say something else happened to you and that was the cause of the injury.

LIE

Your health insurance will send you to helpful doctors.

(**Truth:** You may have to do your own research if you need follow-up care. Make sure that the doctor is willing to participate in an injury case.)

SECRET

Lawyers know which doctors do and do not have good credibility.

LIE

It is okay to sign a release from the insurance company after being severely injured.

(**Truth:** Contact a lawyer before signing anything.)

SECRET A doctor may write a report that blames your medical issues on something other than your accident if they do not wish to be involved in the legal system.

6
No Two Cases Are the Same

There is no certain threshold as to what makes a small, medium, or larger case, and all lawyers have their own threshold and limitations on what they will handle. The best you can do is determine the true extent of your losses and take it from there.

SMALL CASES

A small case is generally a situation where the property damage is an amount that you can successfully resolve with the insurance adjuster on your own or bring to the small claims court on your own. If the initial injury is so minimal that it does not require any medical attention and you do not suffer any long-term problems, then it is unlikely that you need to seek legal counsel to handle your claim. An example of a small case is if someone opened their car door in a cramped parking lot and left a ding mark on your car. You probably have a claim for property damage. The question is: will you go through with the time and trouble to settle this claim?

In situations involving a car accident with minor damage, the drivers sometimes decide they want to handle the damages without involving the insurance companies. I do not recommend this at all. Usually the other party is a stranger, and if police and insurance reports are not made, there is little recourse or consequence if the stranger breaks the agreement. No matter how minor the accident, always contact the police and insurance company immediately.

LARGE CASES

Larger cases come in several different categories. In a case where someone is immediately taken by ambulance and admitted to a hospital, and it looks like their injury will require a long-term healing process, legal assistance will obviously be required. In these larger cases, it is critical to consult a lawyer very early on. Insurance adjusters typically call and demand statements and written authorizations from you that could be detrimental if you do not know the consequences of what you are doing. This is usually one

> No matter how minor the accident, always contact the police and insurance company immediately.

of the worst times for those folks who are injured, want to get better, and are left with loss of income and perhaps loss of transportation.

The next category of larger cases are situations where the injury seems minimal at first but later develops into a more serious injury. These cases end up requiring substantial amounts of medical intervention in order to have a complete medical recovery if it becomes apparent the injury is taking a very long time to heal.

This type of case occurs on an incremental basis. Perhaps at first the accident did not seem serious, and there was no immediate need to go to the emergency room. Maybe there were just a couple doctor visits or a lack of resources in order to obtain medical treatment. People come to our office several weeks, even months, after an accident because they did not even think they would need the services of a lawyer. The problem with these cases where the damages were unpredictable is that it can be difficult to secure the appropriate evidence that was probably easier to obtain earlier in the case.

TRUCKING ACCIDENT CASES

Trucking accidents can be more complicated as there may be multiple parties responsible and multiple insurance policies available to cover your damages. In trucking accidents, involved parties may include the driver of the truck, owner of the truck, person or company that leased the truck from the owner, manufacturer of the vehicle and/or parts, and others.

Since more than one party may be responsible and have available insurance coverage, the process of pursuing an injury claim may become complex. An investigation of the accident scene, the truck involved, witness statements, and a police report will likely be necessary to determine who is at fault. Investigation may also require obtaining the truck's tracking information and any video surveillance that may have captured the incident. It is vital that no property or information be altered or destroyed. Often this requires preserving all information on the accident and notifying the trucking company that you are making a claim. In short, settlement of a trucking case may require coordination and negotiation with multiple insurance carriers and national companies, a task most people are not equipped or desiring to do on their own.

CATASTROPHIC CASES

A case where there has been a death or the injured party is incapacitated requires experienced legal counsel. Unfortunately, these cases occur at one of the most difficult times to make prudent decisions that can have lasting impact. Many well-meaning friends, family members, coworkers, and others may make very helpful suggestions in terms of legal counsel, but the injured person's family may not feel ready to make good decisions. Just remember that the person's judgment you trust in the initial stages of an accident is critical towards locating counsel who can assist in preliminary matters and begin the necessary investigation. If a catastrophic case involves sufficient insurance coverage, filing a lawsuit fairly soon is usually required.

Florida statutes allow four years to file a lawsuit for negligence; however, a suit is sometimes filed early in a catastrophic case because the claims adjuster may not pay fairly if there is sufficient insurance coverage. This is often because the claims adjuster wishes to investigate with their lawyer whether they have any defenses, and they want to investigate you, as the injured person, to see if they can attribute some of your damages to a prior condition or complaint. There are other situations where filing a lawsuit early may not be in the injured person's best interest. For instance, if an accident results in death, the highway pa-

> Florida statutes allow four years to file a lawsuit for negligence.

trol will conduct a homicide investigation. As such, there may be some advantages to wait until the investigation can yield some sort of conclusion.

Deciding when to actually file a lawsuit in court is a decision you should make with your lawyer. It is a decision to make after evaluating the pros and cons of filing a suit early versus later.

WRONGFUL DEATH CASES

Personal injury cases that involve a death are called "wrongful death" cases. This is an exceptionally difficult emotional time for many family members. Wrongful death cases require the appointment of a personal representative to handle all claims on behalf of the person who died because of negligence. This person is oftentimes a family member such as a surviving spouse or parent of the deceased. The personal representative is required by law to bring all claims and can be removed if they are not bringing all lawful claims. It is not required to open an estate and have an executor or personal representative appointed prior to bringing a claim, but it may be required to finish the claim. Generally, it is not a good idea to handle the estate situation before handling the wrongful death matter. Waiting for a meeting with an estate lawyer can cost valuable time, and the evidence you need for your wrongful death case may be lost. Probate operates on different time frames and is not usually considered an urgent issue.

In my office many years ago, I concluded that we could best serve our clients by creating teams for wrongful death cases that could handle both the opening of the estate along with the filing of suit as needed. This can substantially speed up the process and potentially put the survivors of the deceased in a better position. That is not to say that it is wrong to open an estate first then proceed with a wrongful death case, only that it is sometimes better to move quickly and secure key evidence and witness statements early on. Forming a team early to handle necessary estate duties in addition to working with a personal injury team is important and can lead to a better result.

CHILD CASES

Injuries to children due to negligence are heartbreaking. An injured child will have a claim, which is typically brought by their parents. In general, a child has a right to compensation for pain and suffering, permanent injury, or disability in the same manner as adults do. Parents also have a separate right to be compensated for medical bills paid on behalf of the child.

In cases involving children it is particularly important to keep in mind the possible long-term effects the injuries may have on the child's life. In all but extremely minor injuries, it is vital to consult with an attorney.

SECRETS AND LIES

SECRET Never try to handle a car accident on your own with the other driver unless the damages to you and your vehicle are so minimal that you are willing to pay for them yourself. Otherwise, always involve the police and the insurance company.

LIE In a catastrophic case, the insurance company will cover all damages.

(**Truth:** There is most likely not enough insurance coverage.)

SECRET File a wrongful death suit before handling probate.

SECRET You should consult a lawyer in almost all child cases.

7
A Crash Course in Investigation

Investigation is an ongoing process that requires documentation. People do not realize that the initial investigation of their accident is important, particularly if you are unsure of the scope of the injuries you have sustained because of someone's negligence. If it is later determined that you have very serious injuries but the initial investigation was either not done or was not conducted properly, your case could be seriously damaged.

> After an accident on the road, call 911 and request a police officer.

CALL THE POLICE

After an accident on the road, most people know that you need to call 911 and request a police officer. The police officer will write an accident report and may even issue a ticket to an at-fault person. This is an important starting point since it facilitates the development of information at the scene, including all pertinent information about the drivers, their insurance, the types of vehicles involved, and sometimes a diagram is drawn.

It may be helpful to get the contact information of the officer who files the report. This is useful in case you need to contact the officer later. Even though the officer's name appears on the report, it can sometimes be a challenge to read the handwriting.

Additionally, if the at-fault driver is given a traffic citation, that fact can play a role in a determination by the insurance company as to whether they will pay on the claim. Even though this is not necessarily a final determination as to whether a claim will be paid, it is nevertheless very important in terms of the overall case. Accident reports nowadays are available online quickly after an accident so the parties can have a record of the information needed to make appropriate insurance claims. As a starting point, I use accident reports, as do most other law firms, to determine the name of the insurance companies involved in a motor vehicle accident. Accident reports also provide a starting point for interviewing witnesses that may have been at the scene since the police officer completing an accident report may know the name, address, and telephone number of witnesses. It is important that these witnesses be interviewed soon after the accident to determine what they observed.

One of the mistaken notions people make about accident reports is that somehow they will be allowed to be presented to a judge and jury in connection with a motor vehicle accident case. This is not the situation in Florida, as there is something called the "accident reporting privilege," where the information provided to an officer at the scene is not necessarily admissible. Of course, an exception is if there is some type of a crime committed, then information disclosed to an officer at the scene may be used against that person in a criminal proceeding. If a person in an accident is given a ticket for violating a traffic law, sometimes a conviction for this can be useful later in the case in proving that the other driver was the cause of an accident. Oftentimes, a person may admit at the scene that they were at fault, and then their insurance company later claims they were not entirely at fault or not at fault at all.

You should know that even if *you* received the ticket, if the other driver was even partially at fault, you might still have a claim.

> Take scene photos as soon after the accident as possible.

TAKE PICTURES

It is important to have scene photos taken as soon after the accident as possible. Officers that investigate accidents do not typically take scene photos, measurements, or other details associated with an accident unless there is a fatality or one is anticipated.

Photos of skid marks and other indicators that may exist at the scene may be helpful in determining what actually happened. The availability of satellite photos and street-view photos via the Internet are helpful to examine early in the case. Surveying the surrounding area can also determine if there was a surveillance camera operating on a nearby building that may have captured the accident occurring.

GET WITNESSES

Interviewing the witnesses to an accident is important in any motor vehicle or premises case. The memories of various witnesses fade quickly, and it is important to attempt to

Important to keep in mind:

- ✔ File a police report regardless of how minor the accident.
- ✔ Be honest and detailed.
- ✔ Get officer's contact information.
- ✔ Obtain copy of report and send it to your insurance company.
- ✔ Determine if any witnesses were present.

contact them while the information about the accident is still fresh. You may not think that you need to keep up-to-date information on witnesses, but some people can change addresses and cell phone numbers frequently. Since many personal injury cases can take years before they settle or go to trial, preserving those witnesses' contact information and statements is an important component of your case.

I have found that, in some cases, even the person cutting grass nearby is an important witness. Their position as a neutral bystander is valuable in providing relevant information about the case.

ASSESS PROPERTY DAMAGE

The property damage sustained in a motor vehicle accident is important in many cases. The lack of property damage or the total amount of property damage can influence the way that a claim is evaluated by both insurance companies and juries at the conclusion of the case. Having a vehicle photographed and properly repaired following a motor vehicle accident is important to your case.

TAKING MEASUREMENTS

In many types of accident claims, specific details such as the size of skid marks or the precise type of scratches and dents on a car are helpful but not always necessary.

However, decent photographs are useful in demonstrating to a claims adjuster and ultimately a jury the scope of property damage and in making appropriate arguments as to fault and liability. The sooner the photographs are taken after an accident, the better. This ensures that no changes have been made to the area.

For instance, construction activity on a roadway may have been a factor in an accident, and having photos that show that particular scene could be important.

In another instance, if someone steps into a hole on a company's property, their claim may be compromised if they do not have any photographs to show the depth and measurement of the hole.

In claims involving transportation companies, the company often sends their own investigators to the scene immediately after the accident. You probably would not be surprised that their investigation is not generally designed to establish that they were at fault.

REPAIR BILLS

If your vehicle has been damaged due to someone else's negligence, you most likely want to get it repaired or replaced depending upon the circumstances. However, did you know that the actual amount of property damage paid in the claim could be a factor in how the insurance company values your claim? Insurance companies have collected large amounts of information that demonstrate how the amount of property damage in a case can affect the way a jury may assess damages. Oftentimes, if you ask the other person's insurance company to take care of the property damage to your vehicle, they may direct you to their own repair shop in an effort to save money. While there is nothing wrong with letting someone try to save money, you should know that they may not necessarily use the best parts on your car, and there is a secondary objective of keeping the overall repair estimate and final bill low. Since

> Be wary of the insurance company's repair shop. In an effort to save money, they may use low quality parts on your car.

many insurance companies use a computer system that factors the total amount of the property damage into the claim, the cheaper the repair bill, the more likely that you will be impacted both in terms of the quality of the repair and on how your bodily injury claim is assessed.

SECRETS AND LIES

SECRET If your accident evolves into a serious case, it could be damaged if an initial investigation was not performed.

LIE If you receive a traffic ticket, you are at fault. (**Truth:** Even if you receive a ticket, you may still have a claim.)

SECRET

Insurance companies may try to save money when repairing your car, but the final bill can affect and lower your outcome.

LIE

What a police officer says at an accident scene can be used in court.
(**Truth:** The jury does not get to see the accident report.)

8
Don't Let Insurance Companies Use This Against You

If you decide to file a lawsuit or attempt to settle your case prior to suing, it is important to gather all of the medical bills and records in your case. If you have had prior injuries over the last several years, it may be helpful to gather those medical records as well. Sometimes it is easy to acquire completed medical records from the doctor's office, but in other situations it can be a costly and time-consuming task.

WHAT YOU NEED

The process of gathering medical records is an interesting experience. For example, some years ago my father was in the hospital for cardiac care. Knowing the importance of having certain medical records, we thought it best to obtain copies of the records as my father was planning to travel to Florida in the coming weeks. However, upon asking the hospital staff for copies, I was met with a puzzled look. A look that said, "Why would you possibly need to have those?" Even after we offered to provide them with a medical release, the hospital still did not seem readily willing to give us the records. We actually found it easier to have my dad sign a medical release at my law office and fax the medical release to the hospital. It was only then that the hospital immediately provided my office with the records. The system of obtaining medical records should not work that way. Medical records belong to the patient, and the patient is entitled to have a copy. The doctor can charge a sum for medical records, which is set by statute in most states, but it is still complicated to obtain all of the necessary medical records.

The starting point in collecting your medical records is to have an appropriate HIPAA medical release. HIPAA stands for Health Insurance Portability and Accountability Act. HIPAA provides the patient with the right to access their medical records. Despite those rights, medical providers do not make it a priority to provide medical records. I hope that within time electronic medical records will become more common in medical practices and alleviate this problem.

Some doctor's offices may only provide you with a few of the doctor's notes if you ask for medical records. If the notes cover details from the beginning of the accident until the last day of treatment, then sometimes these are sufficient. However, some insurance companies may want a complete copy of everything from prescriptions to out-of-work slips and so on. In addition to requiring prepayment for medical records, some doctor's offices also require that you request the records well in advance of when you actually need them. For instance, some hospitals take well over 30 days to send a copy of medical records.

The cost for medical records varies and is by the page, even if the records are maintained electronically. It can be quite costly to obtain the medical records you need. Sometimes, when the medical provider finally sends out the medical records, the records are not readable and you have to re-request them. This process can take up substantial periods, even if the records are already paid for and are in a fax, e-mail, or download format. The average time that it takes to gather all the appropriate medical records can range from

30 to 90 days in the simplest of cases. If you have treated with a number of doctors, hospitals, and clinics over the years, the cost of recovering all records could be substantial.

In some cases, claims adjusters will want five years of medical records before even making an offer. This might happen if the insurance company database suggests that you have made a prior claim. If you have made a prior claim, then they are unlikely to make any offers until they have reviewed all those records. This may seem unfair and time consuming, but it is all part of the personal injury claim process. The insurance companies know that if you file a lawsuit, then they can send their lawyer to obtain the medical records that they requested from you. Alternatively, if you do not provide those records, then the insurance company will not provide any offers.

Be aware that the request for records is also often a delay tactic by the insurance company, and a request does not always mean that the insurance company is going to make any offers in your case. Oftentimes the insurance company hopes that the statute of limitations will run out on your case or that you or your lawyer will lose interest. A "statute of limitations" places a time limit for someone to file a lawsuit. After the time frame has passed, the injured person will not be able to recover damages, even if the other party was obviously responsible for the accident.

In addition, if there is a wage loss claim, you will need to obtain documentation showing the exact amount of the wage loss with the prior earnings history.

> Be aware that the request for records is also often a delay tactic by the insurance company. Some hospitals take well over 30 days to send a copy of medical records.

WHY YOUR LAWYER SHOULD GATHER RECORDS AND NOT THE INSURANCE COMPANY

In some situations, the insurance company may offer to gather medical records for you and pay for the costs. However, there are several different competing considerations to make before deciding whether to provide the insurance company permission to obtain your medical records. Always remember that the insurance company does not act in your best interest, they do not work for you and you should not provide them with a broad medical release that allows them to access any medical records from anyone at anytime. If your lawyer provides the insurance company with a narrowly tailored medical release with specific medical providers listed, it could save you money. Even though there is a cost to obtain medical records, at least you know that your lawyer is acting in your best interest. In the end, the cost may be worth it and may not even be that great considering the size of the overall case. Also, know that the adjuster will not necessarily provide you with a fair and balanced review of your medical records and the overall impact on the case. They will obtain your personal records and keep them in their database potentially forever, even if they have nothing to do with the case.

Working with the claims adjuster in an insurance matter is somewhat of a double-edged sword, because you (or your representative) need to provide the insurance adjuster with information sufficient to allow them to properly adjust the claim. There is a difference between working with the adjuster and simply turning over the claim and letting them pay you what they feel is appropriate.

For instance, when working with your own insurance company, you have certain duties that you must adhere to under the terms and conditions of your policy. However, before signing any releases for the claims adjuster, it is important for you to know what kind of information the adjuster might require and if that is information that the adjuster may not be allowed to obtain. In a case involving the other person's insurance company, there are significant limitations on their rights to obtain information. The information they use could support your claim as well as be used against you. Bills and records from hospitals, doctors, pharmacies, etc., may contain information pertaining to what insurance is paid on these cases. This is early information that the insurance company does not need in order to evaluate the case. Remember, various types of resources that you may have used to obtain medical care and treatment may have a right of subrogation, and that is not always information that an opposing insurance company should have.

At the end of the day, insurance companies are not compassionate organizations looking out for your best interest; they do not work for you. Insurance companies are billion-dollar corporations that have grown to success by collecting more in premiums than what they pay out.

SECRETS AND LIES

SECRET To start collecting medical records, you must have a HIPAA medical release.

SECRET Some insurance companies may want up to five years of medical records before making an offer.

LIE It is harmless to let the insurance company gather records for you.
(**Truth:** They may gather unnecessary information that can hurt your case.)

SECRET A request for more medical records can be a delay tactic by the insurance company.

LIE The insurance company is looking out for your best interest.

(**Truth:** Remember, the insurance company does not work for you and is looking for advantages against you.)

9
Car Accident Secrets

If you do receive damage to your vehicle and it has been towed from the scene, it is important that you follow up immediately on where your vehicle is located and what the bill will be.

A common misconception is that the other insurance company is going to take care of all of the problems. Over the years, the insurance industry has begun assessing comparative fault in situations involving property damage to a much greater degree. Even if it is a storage center bill, you could ultimately be responsible for a portion of those bills.

If you do not carry collision coverage or if you have a large deductible, the other person's insurance company might not even pay for the totality of the damages. Therefore, it is in your best interest to know where your vehicle is, how long it is expected to be there, how much the accumulated cost is, and how much it cost to tow your car. You should also know where your vehicle is going to be repaired. Similar to any other type of consumer issue involving repair of something damaged, it is best to get multiple evaluations. Generally, we encourage people to consider the body shop that they are very familiar with, a body shop known for the quality of their work, or consider having the vehicle evaluated by a local car dealer who sells the type of vehicle that was damaged. Oftentimes a car dealer who sells the make and model of the vehicle are in a better position to assess body damage, in addition to mechanical and electrical damage on more sophisticated cars.

REPAIR OR REPLACE?

If your vehicle is damaged due to someone else's negligence, the vehicle needs to be evaluated as to whether repair or replacement of the vehicle is appropriate. Unfortunately, if someone damages your vehicle, the law provides that they either repair the vehicle or pay for the fair market value of the vehicle. Even if you have a perfectly functioning vehicle with small problems that you understand and are comfortable with, the at-fault person's insurance com

> If someone damages your vehicle, the law provides that they either repair the vehicle or pay for the fair market value of the vehicle.

pany is only responsible to pay the fair market value of your vehicle.

Therefore, if you owe more money on your vehicle than the fair market value, then being in an accident may end up actually costing you money. Unfortunately, there is no way around this unless you have purchased "gap insurance coverage." Gap insurance coverage is a coverage you purchase from your own insurance company that can protect you in the event your car is worth less than your loan. If there will be a repair on your vehicle, then the amount you should receive will be a combination of the costs of the repair, the diminution in value, and the loss of use of your vehicle during the time it is being repaired.

When someone damages your vehicle, it normally places you in a difficult situation. As many people know, the value of a vehicle diminishes the moment you drive it off the car lot. If you get in a wreck shortly after you have purchased a car, it is very difficult to break even on the repair bills.

RENTAL CARS AND THE LOSS OF USE OF YOUR CAR

If your vehicle was damaged because of someone else's negligence, one of the damages you may be entitled to receive is for the "loss of use" of your vehicle while it is being repaired. This does not mean that the other person's insurance company needs to provide you with a rental car. Even if you have the use of a friend or family member's vehicle during the time that your vehicle is undergoing repair, you still may be able to recover loss of use of your vehicle. Arguably, you should even be able to recover damages for loss of use of your vehicle, even if you do not use a vehicle during the time that your vehicle is being repaired. The amount recovered due to loss of use may vary in certain situations. For instance, if a vehicle belonging to someone under the age of 25 is damaged, to recover the loss of use may require a higher amount due to the difficulty in obtaining a rental vehicle for an under-25-year-old driver.

DIMINUTION IN VALUE

Diminution of value is a damage amount that you may be entitled to from the other driver's insurance company if your vehicle has been in an accident and it is repaired. Diminution in value stems from the fact that, if a buyer were to examine two vehicles, one which has been in an accident but fully repaired and one that has never been in an accident, more likely than not that person would choose the vehicle that has never been in an accident. Some car manufacturers will take cars on trade and place them back for sale on something they refer to as a "certified pre-owned program." However, most of the time when a vehicle has been in an accident and has suffered substantial damage, that vehicle no longer qualifies to be placed into a certified pre-owned program, even if it is repaired. The overall value of your vehicle once it has been in an accident is diminished. Even though this can be a difficult damage to assess, there are experts who work to obtain the type of data that you would need to make a claim against the insurance company. For newer models, a car dealer from a major manufacturer could write a statement for you indicating how much the value of your vehicle has declined as a consequence of being in an accident. Generally, diminished value is not a claim that you are able to make against your own insurance company. You should seek the damage against the other person's insurance company.

This is an important issue; the higher the value of the car and the severity of the property damage often leads to a substantial diminution in value. This damage should be considered in each type of property damage situation.

Most consumers find it is difficult to find legal counsel to assist them in matters involving property damage on a contingency basis. For instance, if the vehicle cost of repair is $5,000, then there is no available additional money to pay the lawyer from that $5,000 since it would need to be paid to the repair shop. Developing this type of detailed information is vital in any property damage claim, so it is important not to rule out any particular type of damage and to get the homework done to present the claim to the insurance adjuster.

MY INSURANCE COMPANY OR THEIRS?

After receiving damage in a motor vehicle incident, you must decide whether to seek payment of your property damage through your insurance company, providing you have collision coverage, or whether you would like to seek payment from the at-fault driver's insurance company. There are many considerations to make before deciding who should pay in the situation. First off, it is important to know if the other person has property damage coverage. The minimum of property damage coverage in the state of Florida is $10,000. If it is obvious that your damages exceed that minimum, then find out if the other person carries more than the minimum of property damage coverage. The at-fault driver may not have any insurance coverage, and we see this situation all too often. Other considerations are the total amount of your deductible, whether or not you carry rental car coverage, and whether there is a substantial diminution in value claim.

If you have a substantial diminution in value claim and the other person has an appropriate amount of property damage coverage, then it may be in your best interest to make a claim against the other person's insurance company, but understand whether the other person's insurance company is going to accept 100 percent liability for purposes of the accident. If the other person's insurance company does not accept 100 percent of the liability, then you may still end up paying a percentage of the car repair costs and rental car costs. Unfortunately, even simple property damage claims can sometimes be problematic.

SECRETS AND LIES

LIE: Someone else will take care of your car and the repair bills.

(**Truth:** You may be left with some of the bills.)

SECRET: The law provides that the at-fault driver either repairs the vehicle or pays for the fair market value of the vehicle.

SECRET You could receive a "loss of use" benefit if you cannot use your car after an accident.

LIE You can make a diminished value claim against your own insurance company.
(**Truth:** You must make it against the at-fault insurance company.)

SECRET You should make a claim against the other person's insurance company, but only if they accept 100 percent of liability.

10
Settle or Sue: Can You Afford to Make a Mistake?

Of course, in most any accident situation you can handle most matters on your own. However, the real question is whether it is in your best interest and if you are willing to risk making a mistake. Generally, if you suffer any type of an injury, it is best to have a conversation with a qualified lawyer to understand the perils and the pitfalls associated with your case. If there is any consideration that your case cannot be settled without a lawsuit, you really should consult a lawyer immediately. Do not be fooled into the false sense that you can settle the case, as it's what you do not know that can hurt you.

Presently, you can bring a lawsuit on your own for up to $5,000 in small claims court, so understand if your damages exceed that amount and the problems associated with bringing such a case. In a case where the damages are minimal, it may cost more to hire a lawyer than what the entire case is worth. It may even be difficult to find a lawyer who is willing to take a case in which damages are minimal and there is little need for any type of medical intervention. However, there is the danger that minimal injuries in the early stages of the case could later develop into a more serious injury. The problem we find is that by the time the serious injury is discovered, many mistakes have already been made in the early stages of the case.

An attorney can help:

- ✓ Review your case and determine how much it may be worth.
- ✓ Obtain necessary documents to help build your case (medical records, police report, etc.)
- ✓ Give you insight into your case and advise you on what steps to take.
- ✓ Negotiate with the adjuster.

HANDLING A SMALL CASE WITH AN ADJUSTER

Cases that allow you to work directly with the claims adjuster for case resolution are typically cases where the amount in controversy is small and/or the amount of the medical bills and lost wages are specific. There are usually not a great deal of the more subjective factors such as pain suffered, loss of life enjoyment, and other noneconomic damages. There are certain types of cases in which it makes more sense to work it out with the claims adjuster. For instance, if someone is injured in a relatively minor accident and their physical recovery is rapid, there are no lingering problems, and there is an easy calculation of any wage loss, sometimes it may be appropriate to work the

> Those who attempt to settle a case on their own may find insurmountable problems later on when they finally seek legal counsel.

claim out directly with the claims adjuster as opposed to engaging in counsel. At the same time, as Abraham Lincoln said, "He who represents himself has a fool for a client." Many individuals involved in a personal injury matter who attempt to settle a case on their own, without understanding the implications of the case, may find insurmountable problems later on when they finally seek the benefit of counsel.

SENDING A DEMAND

In many injury cases, there is an effort to settle the case without filing a lawsuit. The starting point for attempting to settle a case prior to filing a lawsuit is to obtain all of the appropriate records, bills, and documentation for developing a demand letter to send to the insurance company. The decision to send a demand letter depends on the available insurance coverage, types of damages recovered and other factors. The decision as to whether to send a demand prior to suing is often a strategic decision, much like a decision about surgery or other treatment, that should be made in close connection with the medical professionals hired to assist the concerned family.

Sometimes personal injury cases are better settled prior to filing a suit, when a suit is filed the case may actually get worse. There may be information that the insurance company is not necessarily aware of, and filing a suit may allow them to uncover that information. On the other hand, sometimes filing a suit allows the insurance company to be sure that the damages being claimed are appropriate under the circumstances. Sending a demand has its consequences too. Occasionally, sending a demand does have the prospect of settling the case early. However, the problem with a demand to the insurance company is that they often request more information and do not make reasonable and fair offers in good faith. This can sometimes be a delay tactic used by the insurance company.

By way of example, let us say that your lawyer sends a demand to the insurance company on January 1, and there is a continual request for additional information followed by minimal, unfair offers. Then after some months of this back-and-forth, a decision is finally made to file a suit and now you may have lost several months. If the suit had been filed earlier, you would have known that the case would have been resolved as soon as it was able to go to trial. It is rare for insurance company lawyers to attempt to settle a case early on. In fact, some defense law firms rarely engage in any type of settlement discussions until the matter has been placed on the court's schedule and the judge orders the parties to a settlement conference. In some situations, this can take a period of several years, leading to a very frustrating situation for the injured person. In addition, if you file the lawsuit early on, then there are additional costs and attorney's fees involved, which may factor in deciding whether to file a suit or send a demand.

HIGH VS. LOW DEMANDS

The amount of the demand you send to the insurance company will depend on the specifics of your case. Once again, medical expenses, future medical expenses, and wage loss are just some of the main details needed when considering sending a demand to the insurance company, and sometimes the amount of wage loss and future medical expenses can be difficult components to determine.

Wage loss is not a damage that can be reasonably claimed

unless doctor's records reflect that you are unable to work. The doctor records that prove you are unable to work are vital to your wage loss claim. Individuals who have not filed tax returns may face significant documentation issues that can dramatically influence a wage loss claim in a personal injury matter.

Determining past and future medical expenses and wage loss are a starting point and may establish a baseline for developing the amount to demand to the insurance company. There is no fixed formula for how much a jury can award for loss of consortium, past pain and suffering, future pain and suffering, loss of enjoyment of life, and other types of noneconomic damages. Other types of noneconomic damages include significant scarring or disfigurement. These damages can complicate the development of a demand amount to the insurance company.

Since the demand is a negotiated process, an important aspect is determining a value range of the case and asserting a demand as appropriate. Insurance companies use significant amounts of data they have obtained in other cases and oftentimes utilize the opinions of several professionals such as nurses and doctors in predicting the cost of future medical expenses. Therefore, the actual demand amount is a confluence of multiple factors and should be considered carefully prior to sending a demand to settle. It is not generally recommended to make a demand without having absolutely all of the appropriate information in your case.

The claims adjuster will rarely ever settle in the range of your initial request.

When dealing with the claims adjuster, they may ask you what your bottom-line number is to settle your case. This is not necessarily something you should give to the claims adjuster unless you fully understand the dynamics of the entire case. Sometimes this is simply a ploy to establish a lower number than what you first requested; the claims adjuster will rarely ever settle in the range of your initial request. In a situation involving fixed economic loss such as properly documented medical expenses and wage loss, sometimes it is helpful to establish the specifics of those losses so there is no disagreement going forward. When damage is subjective, such as the noneconomic losses or estimations of future medical expenses and future wage loss, there will always be room for a substantial amount of disagreement.

The general rule is to start with a higher demand because you can always come down; it is almost impossible to go up after starting with a low demand. At the same time, a classic mistake is overvaluing the case and creating a dynamic where it is extremely difficult to find any reasonable offer from the insurance company. In fact, studies have shown that people who overvalue prices set for the sale of housing typically end up receiving less than people who makes a reasonable valuation. The same concept can apply to a personal injury case. You may feel like your case is worth a million dollars, but demanding that amount without a reasonable foundation can end up costing you. Negotiating a personal injury case requires a unique understanding of the value of cases

THE COLOSSUS SYSTEM

Most insurance companies are now on a system sometimes known as the Colossus system. This computer system, along with other similar systems, are large databases that contain an enormous amount of information about claims, types of injuries, and a wide range of data factors that are part of your case and others. While the specific details of the systems are held as a closely guarded trade secret by the insurance industry, know that several factors can affect your case. For instance, how quickly you went to the doctor after the accident, severity of the property damage, the number of people that were involved in the accident, the date and time and place of the accident, the doctor you visited, and other factors play an important role in the details of your case.

WHAT IS FAIR?

People who suffer serious personal injuries are often very frustrated that the insurance company does not attempt to be fair under the circumstances. First, there is no specific definition of what is fair. Fairness is somewhat subjective, determined by and dependent upon all the facts and circumstances of the case. Additionally, fairness is something determined by the people on the jury and the judge in the case. What they may believe is fair may not correspond with what you, your friends, and your relatives believe is fair. This can certainly make it frustrating to resolve a claim. Fairness can also vary by the location where a particular outcome of the case is made. What is fair in one case and one geographic area may not necessarily be considered fair in another geographic area. For instance, people in different geographic areas of the United States may have a different outcome for a particular case. If a jury is from an area where the cost of living is higher and wages are higher, then it may follow that the award may possibly be higher. Additionally, some groups of people may be more suspicious than others and consider the court system to unfairly and unjustly compensate accident victims. If the jury pool who will hear your case is drawn from groups of citizens who have that type of bias, it may be reflected in the amount of the award.

Your case may not be ready for settlement until you have completed medical treatment or, in the opinion of your physician, you have reached maximum medical improvement (MMI). This may or may not mean that you have completely recovered; MMI simply means that your condition has stabilized, and no further improvement is expected, even if additional treatment is provided. It is important that you do not settle until your treatment is complete, since once an agreement has been reached and the case is concluded, it is too late to seek additional compensation.

MMI simply means that your condition has stabilized, and no further improvement is expected

SECRETS AND LIES

SECRET Start with a higher demand and come down; it is almost impossible to go up. At the same time, overvaluing your case could cause you to settle for less.

SECRET Do not give an absolute bottom number that you are willing to accept; insurance companies will use that against you.

LIE The insurance company will continually need more information before they can make an offer. (**Truth:** This is usually a delay tactic.)

SECRET The insurance company will always try to settle a case for less.

11
Court Is in Session: When It's Time to File a Suit

It would be ideal to have clear and direct rules as to whether a suit should be filed or not; however, it is a very difficult decision. As I mentioned earlier, as with many decisions involving professionals, oftentimes it is a matter of judgment by the individual professional. In situations where the other party says they did not do anything wrong and are unwilling to engage in a settlement discussion, then the only choice is to file a lawsuit or else drop the case completely.

In many personal injury cases, there may be a time when filing a lawsuit is necessary as opposed to settling the case without a lawsuit. Different lawyers may employ varied strategies and approaches in a particular case. For instance, a suit is more likely to be filed in very serious cases where there are substantial amounts of insurance coverage and a complicated medical liability situation.

In some situations, settlement with the insurance company may not require the filing of a lawsuit. Most people know that by the time the case gets in front of the jury, even if an insurance company's name is not on the lawsuit, that insurance is part of the lawsuit. This is because lawyers do not often sue individuals unless they believe there is sufficient insurance coverage or that person has sizable assets to recover at the conclusion of the case. Particularly if they are working for you on the basis that they will receive a percentage of the total settlement or award. After an initial settlement discussion of the case, if it appears the case cannot settle without a lawsuit, then a suit is filed in the appropriate jurisdiction.

Additional attorney fees and costs that may arise are a consideration when filing a lawsuit at this stage. It is also important to consider what strategic benefits there are from either filing a suit initially or waiting until there is some effort to conduct settlement negotiations. Since settlement negotiations oftentimes involve a substantial amount of back-and-forth, all too often there is a last-ditch effort to settle a case, causing the injured person to reduce the amount of their demand. An insurance company may take inappropriate advantage of that, even though they may have every reason to wish the case moves into litigation. Sometimes the insurance company plans to take the injured person's last, most reasonable settlement offer as an invitation for further negotiations later as the case develops in court.

Oftentimes people find the lawsuit process very invasive as it involves taking depositions of the injured person (perhaps their family's and other individuals' depositions as well) and obtaining other types of information throughout the course of the case. If you are considering filing a suit, first determine if filing suit is going to improve your negotiating position. Next, consider the additional cost and time associated with filing the actual lawsuit. Generally, it may take as long as a year or two before a case actually goes in front of a jury. If either side of a party does not like an outcome, they have the right to file an appeal. An appeal can take an additional seven to eight months while the appellate court receives all of the appropriate documentation and renders a decision.

> It may take as long as a year or two before a case actually goes in front of a jury.

A substantial amount of time and expense is always a component of filing a lawsuit, and filing a suit should not be lightly undertaken unless there is sufficient upside to the value of the case. Sometimes there are hearings before the court, and each one of those hearings have a cost. Since this is part of the case, net cost considerations should be kept in mind. As time has developed, insurance companies have gotten very efficient at handling these cases so that the cost of the litigation is less of a factor for them. Unfortunately, for the injured person such resources are rarely available.

THE PROCESS

The process for filing a lawsuit begins by preparing a complaint that is then filed with the appropriate court. Then the complaint, along with the summons, is served upon the defendant. Additional documents given to the defendant are a number of requests for specific information. The plaintiff can expect to receive very similar questions from the opposing lawyer. The opposing lawyer typically works for or is paid by the insurance company and was hired to defend the claim and attempt to minimize the payout amount at the end of the case. The lawyers will look for every single possible alternative to the insurance company having to pay. They will investigate all of your medical records and history to see if you have had any prior complaints involving the same or similar injury. They will also investigate any possibility that may indicate whether the accident may be partially your fault, as this can reduce what the other person's insurance company would have to pay. The process of filing a suit also involves asking questions to the injured person and possibly members of their family, then ultimately concluding with a trial in front of a jury.

THE COST

Expense of a lawsuit depends upon the severity of the case and the overall cost. There is an initial filing fee, which, depending on the jurisdiction, can run $300–$500. Service of process, presuming it is easy to locate the defendant, may cost $40–$70. Court reporter fees throughout the case can be several thousand dollars. They can charge between $50 and $100 an hour for their time at a particular event. Transcription costs can run three to five times the amount of the hourly charge, depending on the particular court reporter involved. Additionally, doctors charge for their time associated with providing testimony in the case, and sometimes the doctors' willingness to even provide testimony can be a critical feature in your case. Doctors' deposition charges can run from $700–$800 to several thousand dollars per hour with minimum amounts if they are required to provide testimony in a deposition or live court proceeding. The experts can cost several thousand dollars. Many personal injury cases can cost between $15,000 and several hundred thousand dollars, depending on the complexity. Overall, the cost of resolving a dispute with an insurance company can be a very expensive process. In many cases, having resolution of the personal injury matter without the necessity of filing a lawsuit can benefit all parties.

The American system of dispute resolution is considered among the finest in the world but is costly, time consuming, and frustrating for all.

WHY DOES IT TAKE SO LONG?

Proceedings can take a long period of time, such as one or two years. The normal process for lawsuits is:

1. File a complaint.
2. Gather information.
3. The case is placed on the trial schedule with the trial judge.
4. The judge orders the parties to a settlement conference (known as mediation) if the case does not result in a settlement.
5. The case is placed before a jury for presentation.
6. The jury enters a verdict.
7. The judge will enter judgment.

8. Each party has an opportunity to file an appeal to the appellate court.

The process known as mediation is a voluntary opportunity for the parties to discuss the case. Some insurance companies and defense lawyers use this as an opportunity to see how low of a settlement the injured person will go in advance of a trial. While mediation is often helpful, some insurance companies do not negotiate fairly and instead use the mediation process to continue their discovery efforts.

A proposal for settlement is an offer to settle a case for a specific amount. Many people initially think this is a good thing, but generally it is not. Insurance companies have proposals sent to injured people, hoping they will take a small offer on a large case. If you do not take the offer and you do not beat that small offer at trial, you can become responsible for paying the insurance company's lawyer and their court costs. Obviously a very bad outcome from a difficult set of circumstances.

In general, personal injury cases are rarely settled quickly and easily. Anyone who says otherwise either had a minimal case, no available insurance coverage or, at the very least, such minimal insurance coverage that the insurance company paid the minimal limit right away and the case was concluded. This means that either the person was not seriously hurt or they were substantially hurt but there was minimal insurance coverage for the severity of the injury.

Once you send a demand to the insurance company, it is normal for the insurance company to take four to six weeks before responding. Even then, the response may only be a request for more information or an offer so small that it leaves the injured person feeling insulted. This type of response along with the possibility of additional requests for countless amounts of records can cause the case to last a

> Some insurance companies and defense lawyers will use mediation as an opportunity to see how low of a settlement the injured person will go.

substantial amount of time.

Resolving subrogation can also be time consuming, especially when dealing with Medicare, and sometimes resolution of the subrogation interest cannot be completed prior to settlement of your case. You should at least have an idea of the subrogation interest on an ongoing basis, since you have no idea how much is going to be paid in your case. However, Medicare will not provide you with the total amount that they are owed until you have settled your case. Although it does not happen often, I have seen Medicare lien resolution take as much as five years. Unfortunately, sometimes the resource that can provide you the best medical care is also the most complicated to deal with at the end of the case.

Letters of protection are easy to resolve since you most likely only went to one doctor and therefore will only have one medical bill at the conclusion of the case. Nevertheless, there are still other problems with using the letters of protection as I mentioned in chapter 3.

SECRETS AND LIES

LIE If you file a suit, you will receive more money. (**Truth:** The expenses for filing a suit add up quickly. Filing a suit may not always be in your best interest.)

SECRET When you file a suit, the insurance company will launch an investigation and could find out more information about your case that allows them to pay you less.

SECRET Some lawyers believe that mediation is a process to assist the insurance company and not the injured person.

LIE A proposal for settlement is a good and fair deal. (**Truth:** It is usually a small offer.)

SECRET The amount you get for your case is not the amount you can keep. You may owe money towards liens, loans, etc.

12
Surprise! Why You May Have to Give Away Part of Your Settlement

Liens are established throughout the course of a case after using various resources such as medical payments coverage, letters of protection, health insurance, Medicaid and Medicare payments, and lost wage benefits. You may be wondering which liens need to be paid at the conclusion of the case, and what the appropriate amount to repay them is.

In some situations, it is quite clear that the lien will have to be paid in full at the conclusion of the case with very

> Lien amounts should be calculated before you agree to a settlement amount with the claims adjuster.

little room for negotiation. To avoid a surprise at the end of the case, lien amounts should be calculated before you agree to a settlement amount with the claims adjuster. In fact, it may be helpful to include in the conditions of settlement that the injured person resolve all liens and/or their lawyer's satisfaction prior to the complete acceptance of any offer, particularly if there is a large hospital lien that may be difficult to pay out of the available insurance coverage. Once you have accepted whatever settlement has been offered, including potentially the policy limits, the lienholder may be unwilling to negotiate or consider any reduced amount for any reason. This includes limitations of the recovery of the amounts due to comparative negligence or a policy limitation that has influenced the total recovery in the case.

If you are dealing with liens in a personal injury case, it is important to understand the type of lien and the rights available for reduction of the lien since there are many different types of liens, each subject to contract and applicable law that you must follow. For some liens where a statutory reduction is allowed, the lienholder must reduce the lien according to a set formula. However, the law does not provide any rights for reduction for some liens, which is why it is so important to understand the total amount of the lien that must be repaid prior to settling the case. Remember, you do not have to accept any settlement that is offered. It is always your right to take the case to a trial and attempt to make a better recovery with the help of a lawyer. In the end, the only advantage you have in negotiating a lien is the fact that you are unwilling to accept a settlement in which the amount of the lien is greater than any amount you might recover. You must consider that as part of your overall negotiating strategy.

HEALTH INSURANCE LIENS

If you have health insurance and use that as a resource in your personal injury case, it is very likely that the contract of insurance that you pay premiums on has a right to recover all the sums it paid on your behalf. A right of subrogation allows the insurance company to step into your shoes and have a new independent right that allows them to be repaid the sums they have paid on your behalf in whole or in part.

MEDICAL PAYMENTS COVERAGE LIENS

Medical payments coverage, which may be a resource available in both motor vehicle accidents and in premises liability cases, very typically has a right of subrogation and needs to be repaid at the end of the case. As with other insurance coverages, medical payments insurance is subject to Florida law. You should know that you might have to pay back a medical payments coverage lien completely or in part. You may be able to reduce the amount owed by the attorney's fees and costs incurred in acquiring the funds to pay it back from the at-fault insurance company. It is important to have a decent understanding of how medical payments coverage works in terms of an injury settlement before embarking on the settlement of your case. Failing to do so can potentially require you to pay back your entire settlement to your insurance company.

HOSPITAL LIENS

Hospital liens are particularly difficult in the personal injury setting. They are considered a priority of payment, and there is very little discretion to reduce a hospital lien unless the hospital agrees to it. You should understand whether the hospital has a lien on any settlement you might receive, the amount of that lien, and whether there is any prospect for reduction. Be wary that sometimes the insurance companies will send you a check that has the hospital's name on it. This is inappropriate and may lead to some type of action against the insurance company. Hospital liens are recorded in the public record, and it is possible to research and determine if a lien has been recorded timely in your case.

WORKERS' COMPENSATION LIEN

If you have received workers' comp benefits, either by payment of your medical bills or collected wage loss in some form, workers' comp has a right to subrogation as well. The workers' comp lien is subject to reduction according to a statutory formula based on factors such as the attorney's fees, costs associated with procuring of a settlement in a workers' comp lien, and additional consideration for comparative negligence, etc. A bit of a trap for the unwary is that while the insurance company may accept a reduced amount to settle a lien, they also retain the right to recover the unpaid amount of the lien as a reduction against future benefits. This can create a problem with receiving ongoing care and treatment in a workers' comp case since it could require you to pay out of pocket to get treatment.

For instance, if you receive ongoing wage loss benefits, they might be reduced by the percentage amount that the insurance company is attempting to recover from the outstanding lien amounts. If a doctor's bill is $300 for a particular visit, repaying your lien at 10 percent for ongoing benefits, the doctor may ask you to pay $30 of that charge before they will see you. Although $30 may be affordable, imagine if there was a surgery that cost $10,000 and you had to pay 10 percent of that cost because the carrier had already received the lien reduction and had not been repaid the full amount. Technically, you would have received money to pay this, but practically speaking the money may have been spent.

MEDICAID LIENS

Medicaid is a welfare program administered by the states. Medicaid has very severe penalties for not repaying the liens if Medicaid has paid some of your medical expenses. Failure to repay Medicaid can result in a criminal violation. Medicaid may take a small reduction based upon the current statute in effect. Presently, the reduction amounts to a small portion of the lien to account for attorney fees involved.

MEDICARE LIENS

Medicare is part of the overall Social Security program. During your working years, you and your employer have paid a percentage of your wages into the Social Security Medicare system. Paying into the system means that you can receive Medicare if you become disabled or if you receive Social Security retirement. Medicare will make conditional payments on your medical bills, which means they expect to be repaid. However, the amount that Medicare receives is reduced by the amount of attorney's fees and costs that you have incurred while recovering the money that is paid to Medicare. Situations where comparative negligence reduces the overall amount of your recovery can become a problem. Presently, there is no mechanism in place to easily handle this type of situation. Medicare liens can cause substantial difficulties in the conclusion of the case, and it is not recommended to handle a case involving a Medicare lien unless you thoroughly understand how the repayment process operates. In some cases, insurance companies insist to pay the lien directly. If a settlement has been reached earlier and the injured person receives part of the settlement with the understanding that the insurance company is going to pay the outstanding lien amount, this can put the consumer at risk if the insurance company somehow goes bankrupt. If the insurance company goes out of business and Medicare is not paid, then Medicare will come directly after the insurance company, the injured person, and their lawyer.

LOANS AND LETTERS OF PROTECTION

Loans and letters of protection are other bills that are due at the time you settle your case. The interest rates for specific loans are substantial if there are risks involved. There is very little room for negotiating the repayment amount of a loan at the conclusion of the case, and you should carefully assess the potential outcomes of the case if you consider obtaining loans as a resource at the beginning of the case. Borrowing money or services has its consequences.

Situations involving letters of protection are similar. Letters of protection are like a loan from a doctor. A doctor provides the medical services you need with the expectation of being paid at the end of the case. There may not be room to negotiate the amounts rendered on your behalf.

Although some doctors are willing to discuss the payment of outstanding liens at the end of the case, some will not. The amount of a reduction that they may be willing to take is very fact dependent. A common mistake that injured people make, when attempting to handle a case without experienced legal counsel, is taking on a loan that is far greater than the amount they will recover at the conclusion of the case. A similar mistake is receiving medical treatment and care that is far greater than the potential recovery amount in the case. The insurance term for this is "overutilization."

Proper evaluation of a case from the beginning can help you avoid these difficult and frustrating conclusions.

SECRETS AND LIES

SECRET Before you agree to a settlement amount, know the lien amount. Failing to do so may result in you paying your entire settlement to another insurance company.

LIE You have to accept any settlement that is offered. (**Truth:** You can always go to trial and attempt to make a better recovery with the help of a lawyer.)

SECRET Do not take a loan that is greater than the amount you will recover, or receive medical care that is more costly than the amount you will recover.

SECRET Know if the hospital has any kind of lien, some insurance companies will try to send you a check with the hospital's name on it.

SECRET Medicaid has severe penalties for failing to pay their lien; failure to pay can result in criminal violation.

13
How to Hire the Right Lawyer and Avoid Advertising Lies

Choosing a lawyer—the right lawyer—is a very intense and personal process. Typically, people hire lawyers when they are at a crisis point in their lives. They may be scared, angry, and nervous about the future. You will have to share personal information to your lawyer that you may have never shared to others before. Oftentimes you will be dealing with your lawyer for several months, if not years.

Therefore, it is important that you find a lawyer whom you feel comfortable with and can trust to do what is in your best interest. People can become very stressed after an injury, and you can benefit by having a lawyer you can trust to help you make the best decisions. But how are you supposed to trust a total stranger? Where are you supposed to find a lawyer in the first place? The best way to start is to shop around and do thorough research. There is no surefire method to hiring a lawyer that will guarantee the results you are entitled to, but there are some things you should consider as well as avoid.

REFERRAL SERVICES

Referral services are places that lawyers and other professionals pay to maintain a listing. In effect, it is simply another form of advertising. Either the lawyer pays a direct sum or the referral service receives a percentage of the lawyer's fees. These fees can range from a few hundred dollars to several thousand dollars, monthly or annually. Percentage fees can range from 10 to 15 percent of the fees that lawyers receive. This can compare somewhat to the referral fee that a lawyer may receive from referring you to someone else. For instance, you may have a family lawyer who does not particularly handle personal injury cases but may have a friend or colleague to whom they can refer you to for legal work. This legal work would be done on a contingency basis; the lawyer would be paid a percentage of the fees ranging anywhere from 25 to 40 percent of the total amount of money that is recovered by the lawyer on the client's behalf. The lawyer that referred the case would typically receive 25 percent of the fees the case generates. The referring lawyer is supposed to maintain contact with the injured person and has taken some form of responsibility in the case. Unfortunately, in practice this all too often does not occur.

There are a number of referral services that advertise, ranging from television, Yellow Pages, direct mail, Internet, and other media. Lawyers pay to be on referral services, and referral services do not generally maintain any type of quality control standards. Some referral services require their lawyers to maintain some type of legal malpractice insurance, but that is usually the extent to any requirements.

Medical referral services are companies who will refer you to both a medical provider as well as a lawyer and have advertised on a regular basis for many years in the Yellow Pages and on television. If you are considering one of these services, I would urge extreme caution as there is a chance that a poor choice is made with both medical care and with the lawyer. There is no accounting for the quality of care by the medical provider or of the legal advice by the lawyer. This is not to say that there are no qualified medical personnel who receive cases from medical referral services, nor is it to say that there are lawyers who are not qualified to do a good job that receive referrals through medical referral services. However, you should be aware that there are no guarantees, and there are some significant problems in this area, even with referrals from the Florida Bar and other organizations.

ADVERTISING

Generally, advertising and referral services will not ensure the quality of the lawyer or other professional that you may need. Lawyer advertisements have very few indications that can help you decide which lawyer is best suited to assist you.

Over the past two decades, the rules have increasingly relaxed to the point that there is now little meaningful information that you can obtain from advertisements. For instance, most lawyer commercials on television are 30 seconds long and feature the lawyer, a dog, and maybe one person who has been injured. Other than being familiar by seeing someone frequently, it is rare that anyone who advertises on television can impart any real meaningful information about himself or herself enough to encourage you to entrust your case to him or her.

Interestingly, many large television-advertising law firms are nothing more than referral services. The lawyers who are given the cases must pay the lawyer who is the "spokesperson" a percentage of your case. What is wrong with that, exactly? You may think that the lawyer spending all the money on the television advertising campaign must be successful and must make a lot of money, but this is not always the truth. If lawyers need to settle cases to make monthly expenses and the spokesperson (lawyer on television) needs money to pay for more ads, your case could get settled on the cheap and you would not even know it. Sometimes clients are advised to settle their case when, in fact, short-term considerations are not for the clients but for the lawyers. The reality is that many of these firms must have a volume business; otherwise, they cannot survive. In the end, the quality of the lawyer who represents you matters the most and whether they have your best interest at heart.

REFERRED FROM A FRIEND

Referrals from a friend can constitute an important step in receiving solid legal representation. However, know that a good referral from a friend is based upon the specific results of that friend's case. The amount of money they received is dependent on their case's specific details and has no influence on the outcome of your case. The best they can probably tell you is if people were nice, how well they kept them informed, and other more interpersonal qualifications. There is little information that is available that can adequately gauge a specific lawyer's technical skill and tactical ability. Failure to recognize this can cause some difficulties, or at least a poor result.

Many lawyers pay for billboards and other advertisements promoting the amount that past clients have received in their particular case. These ads are somewhat misleading as they only reveal the amount of money recovered by the lawyer, not the amount that the client received. There is seemingly no accountability for the type of case, type of insurance coverage, injuries, amount of wage loss, family structure, and other important factors. The only information given is the gross amount of money that they received, and I have concerns for the individual who chooses a lawyer based on a billboard they saw or an amount they heard about. It has absolutely no bearing on how much your case is worth. Your case could be worth thousands if not millions more than the other person's, or yours may not be worth anything compared to another friend or the person on the advertisement. Ultimately, if you are given a referral by a friend or other individual, listen for more important factors

> Billboard ads can be misleading as they only reveal the amount of money recovered by the lawyer, not the amount that the client received.

that could have encouraged that referral. A quality referral is based upon more aspects than just dollar amount. How responsive was the lawyer and his or her staff to phone calls, questions, and inquiries? Did they have a solid plan for representing you and your case? Did they guide you in selecting the best medical care for your injury? Were they generally supportive and interested? A referral based on these factors is a much more valuable recommendation as to which legal professional can best help you in your case.

REFERRED FROM ANOTHER LAWYER

You may have a lawyer friend that you trust to make a recommendation if you need representation in a personal injury case. However, there are pros and cons to hiring a lawyer based on the recommendation of another lawyer.

A fair question to ask the lawyer who refers you to someone else is, "What's in it for you?" Will they receive a referral fee? You should be deeply concerned if there has been no discussion or mention that the lawyer expects to receive a referral fee in the neighborhood of 10 to 25 percent. Although hiring a lawyer by way of referral can bring you to someone who can excellently represent you in your personal injury case, there is still no guarantee of excellence. Your own research and knowledge about the topic is an important consideration that you should not overlook.

COSTS AND FEES

You have probably seen many advertisements from lawyers and law firms handling personal injury cases where the guarantee is that there are no fees or costs if there is no recovery. However, if you lose a case, you may end up paying for the insurance company lawyer's fees and costs.

A contingency fee typically means the lawyer or law firm will charge you a percentage fee based upon the total amount of the settlement. Sometimes there is some confusion over whether the attorney's fees are based upon the total amount that the client will receive or whether it is based upon the total amount that has been paid in the case. The confusion oftentimes comes about since medical bills and liens have to be paid out of the settlement. Generally, attorney's fees are paid on the totality of the settlement as opposed to what the client will receive.

The costs and expenses in personal injury cases can be very high. If the case is minimal, involves a small injury, or involves a limitation on the amount of available insurance coverage, one can expect that the cost is much smaller, ranging anywhere from a few hundred dollars to several hundred thousand. Cases where a suit is filed can change the costs to exceed tens of thousands if not hundreds of thousands of dollars. Costs can be particularly high if it is necessary to hire a number of expensive experts. Depending upon the case, some experts can charge upwards of $1,000 per hour. As I mentioned before, court reporters are an additional expense as well. Other typical charges are medical copies, postage costs, private investigators, mileage, court filing fees, process servers, electronic legal research, and other matters that can become expensive depending on the case.

I think the best advice when considering hiring a lawyer in a personal injury case is to first truly understand what the cost structure of the matter is and have some solid understanding of the case that you have in front of you and the risks involved. Next, it is important to understand the experience, background, and motivations of all the parties involved in your case. There is nothing wrong with a lawyer who expects payment for their services or reimbursement for the cost they have expended, but if you are hiring a lawyer and have no understanding of the details in your case, then it might be difficult to make an informed decision. You do not want to be surprised at the end of the case.

SECRETS AND LIES

LIE — Billboards and television advertisements offer enough information on the quality of the lawyer. (**Truth:** Most advertisements cannot fully represent the quality of a lawyer.)

SECRET — Lawyers pay to be on referral services, and some lawyers that refer other lawyers will receive a referral payment.

SECRET — If a friend refers you, do not compare their case to yours. Listen for important factors about the lawyer such as efficiency, support, responsiveness, and organization.

LIE

The lawyer on an advertisement is the lawyer who will handle your case.

(**Truth:** You may never even see the lawyer that was on the advertisement other than to say hello.)

14
Assembling Your Legal Team

When someone has been injured in an accident, there are multiple areas of the law that can be involved. For instance, if someone is in an accident while driving from one workplace to another, running a work-related errand, or driving a company vehicle and driving between appointments, then they may have a workers' comp claim. In addition, arising out of that motor vehicle accident they may have a bodily injury claim against the at-fault driver, a claim against their uninsured motorist carrier, and a personal injury protection / no-fault claim. If they are unable to work, then they may have a short-term disability claim and possibly a Social Security disability claim. We often see this sort of situation when someone is severely injured while working on a construction site due to the negligence of another contractor or in a serious motor vehicle accident.

The law has become increasingly complicated due to a number of statutory changes, so there are advantages of using one team from one law firm to handle the diverse areas of the law involved in one accident. There is significant interplay between various areas, and having multiple law firms can cost you since the different law firms cannot see or understand the interplay of the law between practice areas. Some lawyers can be too specialized in one area. Even if you are using several lawyers from one law firm, if they do not work as a team on your case, then they may cost you thousands of dollars.

SOCIAL SECURITY DISABILITY AND WORKERS' COMPENSATION

The interplay between one injury and various areas of the law can be significant. For instance, when someone has been injured on the job and is unable to return to work, they may be able to file for Social Security disability. Once Social Security disability is determined, it can lead to the receipt of Medicare benefits. Because Medicare is a secondary payor, consideration has to be made for the interest of Medicare, and therefore Medicare's approval of your medical settlement is sometimes required in order to settle the case. Additionally, the workers' comp carrier may receive credit for someone receiving Social Security disability benefits. A complete understanding of the dynamics of having someone accepted as disabled in the Social Security system along with the specifics of the workers' comp system are vital to handling this type of case.

PERSONAL INJURY AND WORKERS' COMPENSATION

Many people do not realize that, if they have been injured while on the job, then they may have a separate personal injury case or, if injured while driving, they may also have a workers' comp case. The workers' comp carrier actually has a right to file a lawsuit to recover the money that is expended to care for an injured worker. This is detrimental to the injured worker if the workers' comp insurance company is not necessarily looking out for the best interest of the injured worker. We often find when consulting with a potential client in an on-the-job accident where there are personal injury components (such as from a motor vehicle accident) that the lawyer who has evaluated either the workers' comp case or the personal injury case has not taken adequate consideration of the other type of matter. This can lead to missed opportunities in terms of medical care and the payment of bills.

In one notable case, we found that the workers' comp case had not even been opened, though the injured person was quite clearly on the job. The injured worker came to us after his personal injury protection benefits had been exhausted, and there were no funds left to pay his day-to-day bills. Once we opened a workers' comp case for our client, he was able to receive care and wage loss from the workers' comp insurance company while still maintaining his personal injury case. The coordination of these two important types of claims is absolutely essential in order to maximize the benefits for the injured person, helping them pay their bills and keep a roof over their head.

SOCIAL SECURITY DISABILITY AND PERSONAL INJURY

Personal injury and Social Security disability can play a significant role when someone may not be able to return to work after they have been injured in a motor vehicle accident. When this occurs, it is important to file for Social Security immediately. The time frame for receipt of Social Security disability benefits can range between six months to 18 months depending upon the circumstances of the case. Certainly, if a person is found to be disabled in the Social Security disability system due to injuries from a motor vehicle accident, this is a significant factor in the assessment of overall damage by the at-fault insurance company.

CAR WRECKS WHILE ON THE JOB

When someone has been in a motor vehicle accident while on the job, there is an unfortunate tendency for the lawyer to focus on the particular practice area that they are most familiar with. This is not uncommon; even in the medical field there are doctors who tend to focus on the areas in which they feel most comfortable making a diagnosis, and sometimes this can be detrimental to the treatment of other body parts. In the legal system, when a lawyer is focused on the personal injury aspect, they may focus on sending an injured person to a personal injury protection doctor for ongoing care and treatment. This can be very detrimental in some cases when the workers' comp system could pay a person's lost wages as well as have an unlimited responsibility to pay for medical care.

Of course, all circumstances can be different. There have been some circumstances where the workers' comp system may not be a good first choice given the selection of medical personnel, claims adjuster, or insurance company. Sometimes it is better to look to personal injury protection benefits and/or health insurance benefits as opposed to using workers' comp. When the selection of doctors is limited and the workers' comp carrier is less than helpful, being able to establish a solid treating relationship with doctors who are genuinely interested in the patient is an important component in a personal injury matter. Nevertheless, it is important in many cases where there are multiple areas of the law influencing a person's case that one team is established to handle all aspects of the case.

Lawyers who narrow their practice to a particular area are not necessarily bad lawyers; in fact, some are outstanding lawyers, but it is still important to have a conversation about all the various areas of law associated with an injured person's case.

Another important aspect of having one team to handle all the aspects of a personal injury, workers' comp, or Social Security case is making sure the medical care is completely coordinated. In addition, there is the prospect of conducting witness examinations and potentially discovery depositions with the workers' comp case. This is because the workers' comp carrier actually has an obligation to cooperate with the injured worker, because they have an expectation of being paid back the money that they have expended to an injured worker. This is a very complicated area that is not often pursued by many practitioners in both the workers' comp and the personal injury area. Some of the complications stem from law practices that become particularly focused on one area of the law or the other, and sometimes this can work to the injured person's advantage.

SECRETS AND LIES

SECRET Hire a lawyer or firm that can handle every aspect of your case. You may miss certain benefits if you do not.

LIE You have only one case.

(**Truth:** You may have more than one case, but some lawyers tend to focus on only one area of the law because they do not understand or practice the other possible matters.)

SECRET Find a lawyer who knows the pros and cons of each area of the law and knows how to maximize benefits for you.

ABOUT THE AUTHOR

WADE COYE is the managing shareholder and founder of Coye Law Firm, an Orlando-based practice with lawyers handling personal injury, workers' compensation, insurance, and probate claims among other matters. Coye received his law degree from the University at Buffalo Law School. He holds bar membership in Florida, New York, Michigan and the District of Columbia and is admitted to the United States District Court for the Middle District of Florida, the United States Court of Appeals for Veterans' Affairs, the Eleventh Circuit Court of Appeals, and the United States Tax Court. He has tried cases to a verdict in state and federal court.

Coye's background includes campaign and Capitol Hill assignments for two United States members of Congress and active duty in the United States Army, Infantry.

He was an early adapter of computer technology and the Internet, appearing on one of the first national lists of lawyers using the Internet in 1995. His continued interest in technology led him to develop a custom database for handling client matters.

Mr. Coye, his wife Joan, and five children make their home in College Park. In his spare time, as an instrument-rated private pilot, he enjoys flying and traveling with his family.